Facebook Marketing for Beginners

How to Earn Money While Facebook- king

By: Steven Murphy

9781634289832

PUBLISHERS NOTES

Disclaimer – Speedy Publishing LLC

Speedy Publishing LLC

40 E Main Street, Newark, Delaware, 19711

Contact Us: 1-888-248-4521

Website: http://www.speedypublishing.co

REPRINTED Paperback Edition: ISBN: 9781634289832

Manufactured in the United States of America

DEDICATION

I dedicate this book to my wife Mary. She inspires me to be at my best. From the very beginning, she believes that I can do more.

TABLE OF CONTENTS

CHAPTER 1- THE POWER OF FACEBOOK MARKETING

The Basics

After creating a suitable profile the continuous step of ensuring the line of communication is kept open at all times is important. Positioning the business platform and staying in touch with the viewers will give the site the exposure it needs.

Unfortunate but all so true is the fact that the eye makes judgments' long before the actual material is examined therefore presenting a pleasing file picture is very important as is the follow up information featured.

This is the one chance the posting has to attract the viewer within the very slim window of opportunity.

The wall is the main platform of interaction thus the need to post relevant and interesting content. Keeping this light and entertaining will help to keep viewers come back for more.

However constant alerts may cause an annoyance so striking a comfortable balance is important.

Society now is predominantly more attracted to visual stimulation and this is further broken down into the popular viewing of pictures and photos and other similar platforms when compared to the written word.

Therefore there is a need to explore the possibility of offering a well designed pictorial viewing that will help to enhance the viewer's experience.

Getting into a Facebook group is also another way to create interest in the endeavor being promoted as those within the group are usually like minded or connected to the posting in a more personal way.

The Way You Present Yourself

The following are some of the reasons as to why this may be considered necessary by most:

• As everyone wants to make a good first impression this choice should be given due consideration and be well thought of. The profile picture says a lot about the individual without even having to actually view the written material posted therefore it is very important to capture the attention of the viewer at the very onset of viewing the profile picture. As this profile picture will be viewed by anyone and everyone the choice made must be one that the host is comfortable with. However there is always the option available to change it periodically though unless this is an expected trait of the host it may end up causing more confusion than interest.

• Featuring other elements like logos is also a good idea if the said logo is self descriptive or well known; otherwise this is not a good item to use on the profile. Unrecognizable elements usually do not command as much attention as recognizable ones.

• Keeping the profile picture as simple as possible is also advised as that the element of easy recognition and connections is evident. Thought the element of consistency is sometimes considered boring it can also contribute positively when the profile picture is easily recognized.

• The profile picture chosen should in some way impression upon the viewer the type of endeavor about to be viewed. Therefore it is prudent to judge carefully the perception that the choice will create and eventually the appropriate choice will be made.

Add Friends with Like Interests

Being designed as a social networking site, Facebook encourages the networking between old and newly found friends to add to the list, for the purpose of sharing information, news and other happenings.

People You Understand

Perhaps the first step would be to log on to the Facebook entity to start the search for either old, lost connections or find and make new connections.

Going to the "my friends" page will allow the individual the opportunity to have a quick view of the lists of current friends and some details about them.

Also accessing the "friend finder" tab or "search your address book" will allow for the contact details to be viewed. When all the relevant details are correctly entered the individual's email and password will be able to get the contacts from Hotmail, AOL, Gmail, MSN and Yahoo in the drop down menu phase.

Upon clicking the page featuring the external address book specification will be visible and this will include even those already recorded as friends on Facebook.

The final step would be to then click on those that interest the individual to be requested as friends, upon which the receiving party will either decline or accept the promoting, and respond accordingly.

Once the contact list is made available, writing posting that is individual and personal in its style rather that one format fits all is a more professional way on initiating contact. This individualistic design will help to create the sense of sincerity and honesty. When some form of acknowledgement is evident, thanking the other party for the response is equally important.

Also to be included for maximum social marketing exposure is the posting of material that includes the websites, twitter account, links and any other self explanatory platforms used for the furtherance of the endeavor being touted.

CHAPTER 2- CATCHY IMAGES AND PHRASES FOR FACEBOOK MARKETING

Sometimes mere written descriptions of something will not work as effectively as actually having the visual picture of it. Therefore the use of photo albums and videos can be quite useful in getting the desired message across to the viewers. Posting these on Facebook usually contributes to all the members of the group being able to view and comment on the material being posted.

The Extras

This is especially important if the material intended for posting is also something that is meant to be shared with a certain target audience. There is also the element of convenience whereby all the members of the target audience is unable to view the material at the same time, thus facilitating and catering to this is where the use of photo albums and videos play a part.

Below is a step by step menu on how to feature the photo or video on Facebook:

• Clicking on the video icon or photo icon on the publisher at the top of the group wall is the first step.

• Then the photo should be taken or the video loading started.

• For the photo then posing and following the onscreen instructions while for the video the click should be done on the choose file icon.

• Adding a comment to the photo or navigating the video to the select click and do so.

• The last step would be to select share and this would bring the posting to the target audience intended.

This form of posting is definitely beneficial as it can be considered comparatively cost effective as most of the elements involved do no really require expert involvement.

Using this method to get the service or product recognized by the target audience will eventually help to create the awareness needed to elevate the revenue earning process.

The probability of being able to boost productively is also evident while engaging, educating and selling to the target audience is achieved.

Creating Fan Pages

The creation of the fan pages basically allows for the posting of a separate page for the purpose of facilitating connections between interested parties where information on the latest updates and news can be shared and discussed.

The Pages

This social media too has been able to create the desired effect where other tools have less successful results. Using the fan page effectively is also just as important as the material being featured thus the following guide may prove to be useful:

• The first step would be to start the fan page with the effectively designed photos or logos about the business matter intended to be established. Then adding the contact details of the business to ensure it is reachable in both online and offline circumstances.

• Then the exercise of adding friends and inviting existing customers and prospects to become part of the fan page through links. Once this is achieved to the desired effect then period engagements must be made with the viewing parties. These can take the form of posting new and interesting information or simply engaging in a discussion of the material posted.

• Running other interactive platforms such as asking questions, conducting surveys or simply enquiring as to the likes and dislikes or even requirements of the viewing set.

Functioning as a somewhat free and non committing market survey it can be an exciting way to grow that online business venture. This information gathered can then be used to further improve of what is currently being offered or featured.

The idea behind the whole exercise is to encourage and build a strong following to the fan page by using all the above different incentives.

Constantly encouraging the visitors to become actively participative will also help to eventually create the excitement element that will draw attention to the site. This will then contribute to the possible elevation of revenue possibilities.

Create Events

Facebook has over time been able to establish itself as a power to be recon with when it comes to getting information to the masses. The host of different elements that can effectively be posted and viewed on Facebook has taken many endeavors to higher achieving heights. Almost anything can be effectively promoted.

Benefit From It

There is really no need to promote only events that have exact tangible locations and time lines. The Facebook listed events can also be virtual events as it is able to draw the intended target audience just as effectively.

Perhaps the important guideline to follow would be to make the posting as attention grabbing as possible to ensure the desired outcome. Below are some of the reasons why one should consider using these hosting style events to optimize exposure:

• The reach is limitless when using the events posted on Facebook to get the event noticed. Being able to extend the invitation at the click of an icon and also to be able to add on as and when desired is not possible with other conventional tools. Also being able to add more admits to the event and invite anyone and everyone is definitely beneficial.

• Another contribution this tool can commit to is the easy way it can get an overview of the participants and the capacity anticipated.

• It's also easier to spread the message and communicate to all connected through a single platform effortlessly. Using other complimenting tools like the wall, discussion boards, links, add videos and photos also help to further enhance the communicating possibilities.

One should also note that it may not always be possible to use the Facebook as an ideal way to get events noticed. One of the contributing reasons maybe that there are some people who either don't bother with their Facebook tool or they simply don't have one.

Therefore there may be a need to have emails accompanying the Facebook posting.

Anything exclusive has its positive and negative connective results, therefore it is important to understand the fundamentals that affect such results and then decide if a particular style is suited for a particular endeavor. The use of exclusive landing pages is no exception.

Your Pages

Most landing pages on the Facebook tool helps to create interest in the viewers or fans in order to convert them into being firm fans and this not only raise the fan base listings but also create enough revenue through these interests.

Instead of directly exposing the wall to the viewer one can make a more appealing reach by providing a well designed landing page which is attention grabbing which in turn will be able to hold the attention of the visitor.

There has been verified statistics to prove that landing pages have generated more fans in terms of speed and growth when compared to other tools on the internet marketing arena.

Having landing pages that are exclusive in nature is also beneficial when the idea behind the posting is to not have it "littered" all over the internet thus causing over exposure.

This style of landing pages also creates a sense of exclusivity for the invited guest which in turn most of the time ensures the positive participation of the intended target audience.

Also because the message style is almost always of a singular nature there is little need to have confusing and overly enthusiastic postings.

Using the positive elements of the exclusive landing page will also help to fine tune the different channels of the possible multiple traffic sources.

The different sources of traffic from the exclusive landing page posting may include emails, Ad words, affiliate links, banner placement and others. Using an exclusive landing page is also easier as it does not hamper or cause designing conflicts.

Reward Loyal Supporters

An important part of keeping the loyal element alive and growing lies in the incentives given out as rewards to this perpetual commitment. Using loyalty to gain and keep the business endeavor successful is important; therefore designing attractive rewards for these loyal supporters is well worth the innovative thought process and effort.

The following are some of the more common and rather attractive rewards that most sites use for the reward programs for loyal customers:

• The offer of exclusive discounts, coupons and content material is considered among the most desirable and effective. Tying discounts to other engaging activities will also help to generate interest, revenue and even "free" advertising.

• Using low cost applications to create custom fan only accessible material will also create the necessary incentives that works as effective rewards too. This style of rewards is especially enticing because it gives the recipient a sense of exclusivity that is probably unmatched.

• Giving back is another concept that is much appreciated by loyal fan based visitors. The idea that their contributions are being acknowledged in the form of specially designed rewards is indeed special and thoughtful.

• Designing the rewards to reflect the fact that their contributions are not only important but are also seriously considered for the opinions and feedbacks posted will ensure further long term support. Building the special rapport is a very big and important part of heightening the loyalty percentages.

• Sometimes taking it a notch higher in the exclusivity platform also brings about a pleasant surprise for the fan that is being honored in an exclusive way. This would mean actually featuring the loyal fan by perhaps posting an interview with the said fan where the entire content of the post is about the fan's loyal contribution. This sort of exclusive recognition is beneficial to both parties and to the viewing audience at large.

CHAPTER 3- PUT UP YOUR BUSINESS ON FACEBOOK

Since its launch in 2004 Facebook has quickly become an everyday part of most people's life with over 1.1 billion users and 751 million mobile users there is no doubting the massive impact Facebook has had.

In fact Facebook users spend 700 billion minutes on Facebook a month with the average user logging on for at least 20 minutes a time.

So what does this mean for your business and how can Facebook help you grow your business both locally and wider afield?

The reality is that majority of businesses now have a Facebook page, if they don't then they should have.

If we are spending at least 20 minutes each and every time we log on to Facebook then the likelihood is that we will be browsing through multiple posts and pages, making us a perfect targeted market for your sales promotions and give always, even just for increasing your brand awareness.

With statistics like these Facebook can help you capture your local market but with its potential for huge global reach, you can target new clients further afield, there really is no limitation on your reach.

So how can you capitalize on this and use the power and magnitude of Facebook to help your business grow?

Put simply by using the different forms of Facebook advertising, Facebook has the exposure your advertising needs to capture attention, generate traffic in your businesses direction and help you realize your sales goals.

While the numbers are clearly eye-catching, they are not the only things that make Facebook an attractive marketing source. The social nature of the website is a powerful tool in an advertisers favor as the potential of your posts and ads going viral are massive, that is if you carry them out correctly.

Faceboook Advertising

So what exactly is Facebook advertising well put very simply it's a way of reaching more potential new customers, raising brand awareness and generating sales though the social media platform using a variety of paid methods of advertising all aimed at increasing your reach and sales.

There are different ways to advertise using Facebook; you can place an actual Facebook Ad which runs down the right hand side of a users page.

You can use the "Boost" feature to promote a post from your timeline which will appear on the time line of your fans and their friends this is great for raising awareness of your brand and boosting your number of page "likes".

You can also run an offer or event as well as a sponsored story there are a variety of different methods and trial and error will help you find the best ones for your business needs.

Facebook Ads

Let's start with Facebook Ads; no doubt you will have seen them by now running down the right hand side of your Facebook page.

You will probably also realize that these ads tend to be about your interests, hobbies the things that you enjoy.

This isn't coincidental the ads you see on your Facebook page are tailored to suit you; these are ones that have been chosen specifically for you.

Facebook have targeted these ads for you based on data they have gathered from your Facebook page such as pages you have liked, post you have shared or commented on etc.

Facebook ads are very powerful but they are also very simple. Consisting of a title, text block and graphic or photo.

You have to make sure your ad graphics fit the 110px X 80px Ad space, this is the maximum size it can be to fit that vertical, right-hand Facebook sidebar.

You have to make sure your ads are eye catching and to the point, they can used to promote anything from products and promotions to events and charity listings.

The fact that you can set all the variables for your ad should help you get your ad placement correct making sure you get in front of the correct target market.

So how does your Facebook ad work?

Well let's say you own a cake shop and are running an ad offering a discount on a custom made birthday cake, Facebook will use a demographic tool called insight to collate information on whose time line to place your ad

So they will take you ad and place it on the page of a mum of 3 for example, who has perhaps liked or commented on children's birthday and party posts before, who mentions her kids on her profile and page.

This is because the chances are money off voucher for a birthday cake is likely to capture her attention and be something she is interested in.

The Down Side of Facebook Ads

Like any system, Facebook Ads has its own drawbacks: Some of them the same drawbacks you'll find in any online advertising system, and some unique to Facebook. Let's take a detour and make sure our eyes are opened wide to the dangers. While it's true that as a form of pay-per-click (PPC), a Facebook Ad can reach a more tightly-focused demographic and cost considerably less – partly because mainstream marketers haven't yet discovered the potential waiting to be mined – it is nevertheless possible to rack up costs pretty quickly! One way to combat this: Have a daily budget, and set limits.

There are also rules and restrictions you need to keep in mind, so before deciding to create your Facebook Ad, make sure you thoroughly read the guidelines. These guidelines are broken down into sections:

• Accounts

• Landing pages/Destination URLs

• Facebook References

• Ad copy and Image Content

• Prohibited content (a large section!)

• Data and Privacy

• Targeting

• Prices, Discounts and Free Offers

• Subscription Services

• Ads for Alcoholic Beverages

• Copyrights and Trademarks

• Spam

• Incentives

• Downloads

This page also contains a list of exclusions and formatting rules you need to observe, if you're using the Facebook Platform. There are ways to legally and ethically work your way around some of the restrictions; others are absolute.

For example, one of the general restrictions is: "No contests or sweepstakes", but Zynga got around this by simply asking Facebook's permission, and following the Promotion Guidelines for permitted contests. There are other rules in which you simply have to present your case to Facebook:

1. No multiple Facebook accounts for advertising purposes unless given permission by Facebook

2. Advertisers can't automate account or ad creation unless given permission by Facebook

And some that are absolute: For example...

1. Ads that contain a URL or domain in the body must link to that same URL or domain.

2. Ads must send users to the same landing page when the ad is clicked.

Do remember that if something is not self-evident, or your particular set of requirements goes outside the norm, you can always talk to the sales team in person, to see if there's a way you can both make what you want to do work. (After all – they want your money!)

9 Facebook Ad Mistakes

There are definitely ways to reduce the effectiveness of your Ad on Facebook, and here we will take a look at 9 of the most common...

1. Assuming that all Ads are created equal. Facebook selects Ads to repeat based on the best performers – the ones that generate the most click-throughs or impressions. That's why it's important to support your Ads with interactivity-promoting tactics such as having a Facebook Fan page, and making sure you really do target the right people.

2. Not tweaking your Ad as your campaign progresses. Too many people create an Ad – and leave it. Even the best, most professionally optimized Ads go through a natural cycle of peaking and declining activity, so make sure you monitor this, and adjust your ads as needed. (Facebook is also more likely to keep displaying your Ad, if it sees you are keeping it current.)

3. Not putting your Ad in the best Facebook category. To figure out the right one, you need to think like your viewer: How would she categorize your product? You may think of your custom-embroidered hemp pillows as "home décor accessories"... but your ideal customer might be looking for "green products".

4. Picking too broad a category. This is a mistake usually born of inexperience. No, it's not better to reach 1,000,000 readers in the hope that a handful might actually be interested in your Ad subject: It's better to narrow your focus to an exact, small target group – one that will give you comparatively higher conversions (sales).

5. Not reading all the guidelines and restrictions. That one should be obvious, but still trips potential Advertisers up all the time. The best way not to "miss" something is not to rush through the

process. Read the guidelines and restrictions first – do your homework!

6. Rushing into Ad creation. See # 4... and make sure you've thought of all the ways you can maximize your Ad dollars. Have a plan; don't just fire your canons off in all directions. Think through your campaign, and plan for the long term (and for modifications) too.

7. Putting all your eggs in one basket. Especially if it's the first time you've advertised on Facebook, it's best to start small. Don't commit your entire Advertising budget to it (unless your budget is miniscule – a tiny budget being another "mistake", but sometimes, one that's unavoidable for new marketers.)

8. Not realizing you need to link your Ad to page, event or group on Facebook. The purpose of the Ads, as far as Facebook is concerned – publicizing and promoting Facebook. So even if it's your own website you want to promote, your Ad should to direct people to your Facebook page, event or group for your website.

9. Not carefully checking formatting and spelling. Make no mistake – you can easily get your Ad disapproved by using poor grammar, unprofessional formatting or having spelling mistakes.

The Privacy Issue

We've already skirted around this by discussing the Beacon fiasco. Facebook has been criticized heavily for privacy infractions; not all of which are now corrected.

The truth is privacy is something you can't take for granted in any area of the internet, these days. Nor can you be responsible for people who don't take the time to check privacy settings on public sites, or take the time to institute any parameters they wish to set. As long as you too create your Facebook groups, events, pages and ads in good faith, taking care to follow ethical and sensible practices (and pick your categories and target viewers carefully, after proper research) yours won't be one of the business to suffer from any lawsuits.

Speak to just about anyone you know (especially young women under 39) and you'll most likely find that Facebook's popularity seems to outweigh

4 You can read a comprehensive summary of Facebook's past privacy problems at Wikipedia its drawbacks. This makes Facebook an important venue that should not be ignored, when planning your Advertising campaigns. I hope that this guide was very useful to you and that you are ready to harness Facebook for your marketing campaigns. The most important step now is to take what you have learned from this guide and take action. Go login to Facebook now and start implementing the free techniques that you learned and start building a few Facebook ads campaigns, I am sure that your online business will quickly pick up and fly through the roof.

CHAPTER 4- THE DEFINITION OF FACEBOOK CPC

CPC, stands for "Cost-per-click", is a way of advertising where if someone clicks on an advertisement that they see via a site such as Google or Facebook then the business pays marketing the marketing company for each click.

If the Ad gets no click then you don't pay a penny but you still get some exposure.

Facebooks CPC option works in a very similar fashion to that of Google AdSense PPC campaign, in that a business or individual can bid on keywords that are related to their business.

If you win the bid for your preferred keyword then you agree to pay "x" amount of money for each click.

How to Use Facebook CPC

All you need to do in order to get started is again go "Create an Ad", very much as before however this time you will choose the option for Pay per Click

Next is the "Targeting" section of the form. This section is what really makes Facebook PPC worthwhile. With "Targeting", you can actually choose who you want to see your ad based on a number of factors, such as:

• Age

• Gender

• Marital status

• Facebook "interests"

• Service area

As you narrow down your target market, Facebook will give you a general idea of the number of users who will be targeted with your campaign

You have two budgeting options: a lifetime budget, or a daily budget.

The lifetime budget will send the max amount of traffic to your site in the least amount of time possible.

The daily budget will send traffic to your target site just a little bit at a time until your Facebook campaign is over.

Is Facebook CPC Worth It?

You're essentially paying Facebook to find leads for you that you didn't even know were out there, It's expensive and can large sums of money but for the potential reach you get in return it can be very worth it!

What is CPM?

CPM stands for cost per 1,000 impressions. In other-words you pay whenever anyone sees your AD

When you set up your ad on Facebook, It will show you how many people are expected to see your ad in other-words the impressions range of your ad say between 3,000 and 5,000 for a $20 budget.

So if your goal is to get more likes for your Page, your ad will be shown to people in your target audience who are most likely to also like your Page.

However you pay once your number of impressions has been reached and your budget spent even if very few of those impressions actually clicked on your ad and came through to your page!

Is CPM Worth It?

Again it's like all advertising on Facebook it will depend on how you run your campaign however it can be easier to set up than CPC and can be less expensive but the ROI can also be less and you pay regardless of whether they come through to your page or not.

How Does Facebook Targeting Works?

Targeting on Facebook has changed as of April 2013 it now gives advertisers more options to narrow down their target market which should essentially give a better ROI.

Here is a brief run through of your targeting options Geographic Location: You can target your advertisement to people who live in a certain country, state, city or post code. You can also choose cities near your chosen location within a 10, 25 or 50 radius.

Age: Select the age range that is most appropriate for your business and the content you are promoting there is no point in putting your ad in front of people who are the wrong age demographic.

Gender: Is your target market mostly men or women? Or, is your target market men, but women also contribute to the buying decision? You can select them both or just one.

Interests: The KEY to Facebook Advertising. You can select certain interests to ensure that your ad is placed in front of the right audience.

For example, if your product is children's clothing, you can target your ad to Parenting, Family, Kids, Kid Activities, etc.

Connections: You can show your Facebook ad to anyone, people who already like your page, and people who do not yet like your page.

One of the most successful is friends of connections as this option shows your ads to friends of your existing fans. For example, "Carolyn likes Digiscot" or "Daniel likes Scotland FC."

People value their friends input when it comes to purchases, likes etc. so this method can yield great results.

You can also look to target: Education Targeting, Age and Birthday Targeting and even Mobile Device targeting for those most likely to view Facebook Ads from their mobile or tablet computer!

These targeting options now make it so much easier to get a high level of ROI from your Facebook ad!

Chapter 5- How to Properly Execute Your Facebook Ad

Of course you need to do more than just create and pay for your Facebook Ad, It's vital that you thoroughly research your competition and your market, maximize every possible advantage that's ready and waiting for you if you can utilize Facebook's powerful social-oriented platform.

Have clear set goals before you set your ad, think about who you want to target, what are the key demographics, what are their likes and interests what are their personal circumstances are they married, do they have kids?

Then think about what it is that you are going advertise, do you have a seasonal product or service you wish to promote, is it a special offer you are promoting or a new range of stock.

The next thing to plan out is what you hope to achieve from placing your ad.

Are you looking to increase likes, do you want to generate sales and if so then what is your sales target, are you looking to raise brand awareness?

Decide how long you want your ad to run for and how much you want to spend work out the maximum daily advertising budget you can afford to spend and don't be tempted to stretch yourself to a higher daily budget than you can afford.

You need to have clear advertising plans and goals in place before you start and that will help you achieve the best results from your advertising.

Also bear in mind that It's not enough just to create Ads for a webpage. You want to make sure you get the most out of your Advertising dollars by maximizing Facebook's platform in as many diverse areas as possible.

The more interactive your Facebook Page is the more successful your ad is likely to be especially if you can keep people engaged in your page longer than just the duration of your ad.

This brings us onto the subject of Facebook fan page and "likes" and where and how they relate to your Facebook page and Facebook Advertising.

When it comes to Facebook fan pages one of the key elements of your pages reach is the number of "fans" your page has in other words the number of likes your page has.

Now when it comes to likes only likes from personal pages increase your like counter, If a business page likes you then it doesn't increase your like count but they will still see your posts and updates and are of course still potential clients.

Now a year ago fan page owners were obsessed with increasing their like counter and you could easily go onto a website such as Fiverr and buy hunderds of likes for your fan page making it appear very popular.

However there were many problems with this method of gaining likes. The main one being they were "empty" likes in that other than increasing your page likes it really did very little for your pages interactions and was not going to bring your page any business.

Then Facebook clamped down on fake likes and removed them from pages, this was a good thing as it encourages page owners to cultivate genuine likes from people who are likely to interact with the page and therefore increase its reach and become potential new clients.

Of course Facebook Likes are only one part of the equation you need to make sure that people who like your page are interacting with you.

Make sure the posts you put on your page encourage others to participate in it through commenting on the post, liking the post or even sharing it to their own page.

The key to making sure your Facebook page is effective in terms of likes and interaction is good networking and making sure your Facebook fans are connecting with your page, the more effective your Facebook page is the more effective your Facebook advertising will be.

So how can you tell if your Facebook page is working effectively, this is where your Facebook admin panel on your page will come into effect? It is here that you can keep up to date with your pages stats and see what's working and what's not. In this section of your page you can see an over view of your posts and any messages your page may have, you can also invite friends to like your page and place your ad from here.

One of the key ways to build relationships and interaction on your page is to join any community pages that relate to your page so say for example you run a craft page, then you could join a community craft page to build relations and increase likes to your page.

Another way to drive traffic to your page and increase likes and interactions is to run a competition from your Facebook page. In this next section we will go over some of the key points when it comes to running a competition on Facebook.

Effectively Run a Facebook Contest

A Facebook competition is a great way at driving traffic towards your Facebook page, it can be a very useful advertising resource for your businesses but you have to make sure you do it correctly as there are whole list of Facebook rules when it comes to competitions.

Here is a quick list of the things you can't do with regards to running a Facebook competition:

1. The product or service you are promoting has to be yours, either as an authorized merchant or the manufacturer.

2. You are responsible for ensuring your contest does not break any laws, rules or regulations and you must clearly state the official rules, offer terms, and eligibility requirements.

3. Promotions must use Apps on Facebook and state that Facebook has nothing to do with the contest.

4. You can ask entrants to Like a Page, check in to a Place, or connect to your App when they enter the contest, but that action cannot automatically enter them. You cannot ask them to take any other action on Facebook, like leaving a comment on your wall.

5. The Like button cannot be used for voting.

6. You cannot notify winners through Facebook in the first instance (you need to notify them via email phone etc. first then you can post it on Facebook).

So now we have covered the don't s when it comes to Facebook competitions what are the Dos.

Have a goal: Whether it's more Likes, increased brand awareness, new product promotion, better user engagement, etc., have a goal so you can measure whether or not your contest worked.

Make it interactive: A fun, interactive experience will draw more entries and encourage word of mouth and social sharing.

Be creative with contest prizes: Your contest prize can be something with broad appeal – a gift card to Amazon – or niche appeal – a private sewing class. Whatever you decide, make sure it appeals to your target audience.

Choose a third party App that is easy to use: Look for one that is customizable, cost-effective (some are free), and mobile-friendly and that can be embedded on your website.

Make it easy to enter: Ask for the bare minimum amount of information from entrants (like name and email), and make it easy to enter, like answering a trivia question or uploading a photo of a pet.

Follow up: Once the winner is announced, follow up with the entrants by responding to feedback or simply thanking them for becoming a part of your community.

Facebook competitions are great for driving traffic to your page and for raising awareness of your business and your brand but they can also be great for generating sales and making money.

For example, say you run a competition offering 3 months SEO and you ask people to for their name and email address, you let the competition run for two weeks and during that time 250 people enter the competition, At the end you pick one winner and then what are you left with?

Well you now have a list of 249 people, who you know are looking for SEO for their business, you also have all of their email addresses so you send off an email saying:

"Sorry you didn't win this time here is a voucher for £100 off any SEO package in the future and don't forget to like our Facebook page for any further competitions and special offers.

Then you will find that some people will take up the discount offer then and there (they were already in the market for SEO that's why they entered the competition).

Others might like your page and become a customer in the future and to top it all off you now have an email list of potential clients who are interested in SEO services for their business.

CHAPTER 6- HOW TO CREATE FACEBOOK OFFERS

As is the case with the Facebook competitions, Facebook offers are another great way of generating traffic to your Facebook page, raising brand awareness, compiling a responsive mailing list and of course the most important thing a Facebook offer can make you money!

As with all other forms of Facebook advertising and promotion you really need to think about what you are going to offer, who you are going to target, when you plan on running your offer and the outcome you would like at the end.

Offers are a fabulous way of making sales; you can offer a monetary discount or a % off your product or service. You could offer something free such as buy one get one free or even just free postage.

You could make it a time sensitive offer to encourage people to snap it up or you could limit the amount available to create a feeling of demand and urgency.

Making it as attractive an offer as possible will encourage others to not only take up your offer but to share it on their page.

The more buzz you can create for your offer the better.

You want it to be irresistible to people, you want them to want it themselves then show it to their friends as well, making it a viral offer.

However Facebook plan on phasing out the Facebook offers option from last summer of 2013 and instead you will place your offer as an ad this is being done in a bid to streamline the number of ad options available so that they can be reduced down from the current 27 options available.

This is to try and make things less complicated for businesses as a number had already started to just us the "place Ad" feature to run an offer instead of the offer option itself.

Sponsored Stories

Sponsored Stories are built around user activity. Advertisers simply pay to highlight an action that users have already taken on the social network or within a Facebook-connected app. That action is shown to a user's friends, either in the sidebar or in News Feed. Sponsored Stories cannot be used to reach an audience that is not connected to the page or app through a friend.

Promoted Posts

A Promoted post on Facebook is a post whereby you pay a sum of money at a CPM rate (cost per thousand views) to increase the number of people who see it.

These promoted posts will last three days and during that time period your promoted post will continuously show up in the News Feed of your community members and their friends pages.

Visual posts such as pictures, graphics and videos receive much more engagement than plain text posts, they are more eye-catching and more likely to capture people's attention, where possible include some sort of call to action.

You want to get the best return for the money you are spending by promoting a post; therefore it makes sense to use an eye-catching visuals in your promoted post.

As you are paying for the post it is essentially becoming an ad, and therefore it's advisable that you as with track the ROI as you would with other types of advertising.

Again have a budget in mind when it comes to "boosting" your post, the budget you set will determine how many people see your promoted post, however your budget can also be increased during the three days if you think you are getting good results and want to extend the posts reach even further.

Facebook Edgerank

There has been a lot of chat in the world of Facebook about how Facebook's algorithm Edgerank is affecting pages post reach and what impact this is having on the pages of business owners.

Firstly what is the "The EdgeRank Algorithm"

According to Facebook this algorithm is the sum of Edges, each Edge is made up of Affinity, Weight, and Time Decay.

I'm going to take a guess though and say that might just have been as clear as mud! If that's the case don't worry it's really not as complicated as it sounds when you begin to understand the underlying concept, it's actually a simple and effective algorithm. The first thing to clear up is what exactly Facebook mean by an "Edge".

An Edge is basically everything that "happens" in Facebook. Examples of Edges would be status updates, comments, likes, and shares.

Basically any action that happens within Facebook is an Edge. So what then does EdgeRank do?

EdgeRank ranks Edges in the News Feed. EdgeRank looks at all of the Edges that are connected to the User, then ranks each Edge based on importance to the User. Items with the highest EdgeRank value will typically go to the top of the News Feed.

Edgerank takes into account the affinity, weight and time decay to decide upon an edges value to a user.

Affinity is a one-way relationship between a User and an Edge.

Essentially how close of a "relationship" a Facebook Page and its "Fan" may have. Actions such as Commenting, Liking, Sharing, Clicking, and even Messaging will build the Affinity between the page and the fan and the more frequent this is the more value will be given to the affinity rating.

Weight is a value system created by Facebook to increase/decrease the value of certain actions within Facebook. Commenting is more involved and therefore deemed more valuable than a Like.

Time Decay refers to how long the Edge has been on a page; the older it is the less valuable it is. This helps keep the News Feed fresh with interesting new content, as opposed to lingering old content.

So what does Edgerank mean for your Facebook page and your Facebook advertising plan?

Well it's nothing to be scared of like a lot of businesses seem to be. It merely emphasizes the point that you need to keep your page up to date with interesting content that encourages your page's fan to be drawn in to communicate, the more interactive your page posts are the better they will do when it comes to Edgerank value.

Chapter 7- 8 Essential Information to Remember for Facebook Marketing

Step 1: Pick Your Topic... Identify your target market...

Step 2: Create a Facebook Page Account... the right one...

Step 3: Create your cover image... not breaking the rules...

Step 4: Create your profile picture... avoiding confusion...

Step 5: Create the "About" section... engaging the visitor

Step 6: Using Facebook tabs... absolutely amazing...

Step 7: Posting... getting the most out of it...

Step 8: Getting "Likes"... quickly and safely

Step 1: Pick your Topic... Identify your target market...

The first thing you need to do is clarify what your business is all about, what your brand is, and what your purpose is in the marketing world. The following questions will help you to clarify and understand what the marketing vision of your business is all about.

What kind of people are you trying to reach? I'm really sure you already know the type of people that your services are directed to. You see them constantly, they contact you as well if necessary, and that will tell you what kind of person are they and how you can treat them.

What do they look like? Are they fat or skinny? Male or female? Old, young or middle-aged?

What are they looking for? What is the final goal they are after based on the service you provide? What feeling are they trying to reach with it? Do they need it to feel happy? Do they need it to survive? A lot of needs must be taken care of for a person to survival.

What do you actually do for them? Maybe you are already offering a service for that audience. That will give you a great vision of what exactly you need to inform any new people that fit into that same audience.

What kind of information would they be interested to know about and pay for? You already know the needs of your customers; you know exactly what kind of information will be highly helpful to them in order to help them to satisfy those needs. Why don't you just create a great info-product about it?

How much money are they actually paying you for it? Knowing how much you usually charge them for your service is a very important indicator, because if you decide to create a product like a report, a video training, software or something directly related to your audience, you may simply be able to figure out the price tag you can easily stamp to it.

How would they like to reach that content? Is it Video, Audio, Written, or Blogging? This is important to know. You may just think about it. Think on their limitations to read, hear, watch or use the computer. If they can do everything you can just ask them what they would like to know about stuff. Do they like to read? Do they like to watch videos? Do they like to hear audios?

Where are they from? Maybe you have an audience that comes from other cities or even countries. That will happen a lot on Facebook. You need to target every one and adapt your information to all of them at the same time.

What are your competitors offering to your audience? In the marketing world it is very important to study the competition that targets your exact audience. What do they generally offer? What things do they offer that you don't? Do they have more clients? Do they work additional hours? Do they cover a lot more needs than you?

Can you offer a better service/product than your Competitors? Once your know everything about your successful competitors you can just offer the same thing, but with your personal touch plus a lot more great things that they are not offering. You can have special offers, free samples, free call consultation, special discounts, etc.

These questions are very important in deciding how to establish your business over Facebook. You can position almost any kind of business over Facebook because Facebook is more than just a website or a service; it is a large audience of people with real human needs who are waiting for you and your service to satisfy them.

Step 2: Create a Facebook Page... the right one...

There are many categories you can base your Facebook Page on. This is a very important section because it will be the beginning of something great for your business, and it is essential that you do it correctly.

The category you select here will define the "Type of Page" you will create for your business on Facebook.

There are 3 important things you should know before going on to the next step of the creation process:

1. The Category. You will be able to edit your Category at any time inside the administration panel.

2. The Page Name. You will able to change your Page Name only if the page has fewer than 200 likes, after which you won't be able to change it again.

3. The Facebook Pages Terms: Please carefully read the Facebook Pages Terms so that you don't break any rules and Facebook doesn't shut down your page at any time. It's short enough, so please read every word! Check this little box once you have read the terms and then click "get started."

Here you have two options. Either you can login and install your Facebook page inside of your personal Facebook account, or you can create a new and separate business account exclusively for your Facebook page. I chose the first option because it is easier.

Now the process will lead you to set up the "About" section. You can add the URL of your website now, and you may also inform Facebook if your Facebook Page is a real organization, school or government.

You can add it now but I will be talking about that later as well, so click on "Skip" for now.

Finally, you will be able to add what is called the Facebook web address. This will give a great search engine buzz to your Facebook page because the address will be treated as an original Facebook page by search engines.

This is where I must give you some very important advice. I strongly recommend that you find a unique keyword to use as the web address for your Facebook page. If this is a page for your offline business, simply use the name of your company.

If it is about a topic, you can use various freely available keyword tools on the web to perform keyword analyses and pick phrases which people search for often. I recommend Google Keyword Tool. https://adwords.google.com/o/KeywordTool

Once you find your unique keyword, you can use it as your Facebook page name as well.

Now you can do two things: you can go right now to the Google Keyword Tool and find a unique and highly-searched keyword, or you can just click on the "skip" button for now and do it later.

If you do it now, the username will be set up instantly, but if you decide to do it later you will need to have 25 likes before the username is set up. Either way, you will only be able to change that username once.

Because Facebook knows your page is brand new, it will prompt you to set up your payment information so that you can start advertising right away to get "likes." You can do that later, however, because we need to take care of some other things before we begin advertising. Click the skip button.

Now you are done with Step 1. Let's go to the next step and create the cover image for our brand new Facebook page.

Step 3: Create your Cover Image… not breaking the rules…

This will be the first thing your visitors will see once they get to your Facebook Page, so for that reason you really need to be really good at it so people may get an appropriate first impression.

There are some extremely important tips you really need to be aware of on creating your cover image:

People will need to see what your Facebook Page is all about in just a few seconds.

Avoid the use of call to action or any kind of advertising material in your cover image. Facebook don't like desperate advertisers using their services at all, so be aware of that and use only images to get people to know what your Facebook page is all about.

Use images that show what your clients or customers really want, show the end result of your services right there in front of them. Just sell the benefits using images and not words at this spot.

Steven Murphy

Use colors related to your company logo, product or any other kind of object you would be working with in order to satisfy those needs. Everything will need to be related to what you are offering or selling.

If you have a website related to your business or services, it will be a great place to put the address right there in the cover image, as that will tell what that Facebook page is representing online.

Step 4: Create your Profile Picture... avoiding confusion...

It is a great place to locate your logo, product or a photo of yourself.

If your Cover Image doesn't show your logo, the profile picture should be the place where you should place it.

If your cover image already shows your logo, you may use the profile picture to show your main product.

The images should be clear and not confusing.

And of course it should relate to the principal colors you are already using.

Avoid the use of long phrases or text that is hard to read, or the size is too small to put a text that is smaller than a logo.

Step 5: Create the "About" section... engaging the visitor...

This is where you will be able to explain in a few and simple words what your business or service is all about.

You will have only 150 characters to show in this spot. Inside of it you will have a lot more space to write, but that small portion will be what everybody will see first and most of the time the only thing they will read as the description of your Facebook Page.

For such a small place you should be really wise in choosing the words you use to grab visitors' attention quickly.

If you decide to include a URL you can do so. You usually will put your domain name here, but if the URL happens to be too long, we advise you to use a shorter URL.

A really cool advice here is to approach the reader more than yourself.

You just need to click in the "About" link. Then you click on "edit." That will lead you to the "Basic information" interface. Write the information on the "Short Description" box. Include all your business information as well, but concentrate on the "short description" one. Finally, after you are done go down and click on "Save Changes."

Step 6: Using Facebook Tabs... absolutely awesome...

Facebook Tabs is where we may use an incredible arsenal of high technology marketing tools called "apps" that will convert your Facebook Page into more than a regular page. Facebook Apps are additional places where you may store highly useful places where people can enter and know more about special deals and information.

You may have a great set of additional pages with awesome functions all inside Facebook, so people don't go outside of your Facebook Page to interact a lot deeper about your business.

There are all kinds of Great Facebook Apps that you may use with amazing functions to be enjoyed.

You may install a new App to your Facebook Page by simply searching for one by typing in the search bar, but remember to do it using your personal Facebook profile interface.

Step 7: Posting... getting the most out of it...

This place is where we will do all the magic here on your Facebook Page. And let me show you all the amazing things this really cool box is capable of doing. I will explain 5 highly effective functions that this amazingly powerful little box has to offer to you and your business:

1. Facebook News Feed:

Once you post something into your Facebook Page every single person that has liked your page will receive that same post into their own Facebook Personal Account "News Feed."

The Facebook News Feed is:

1. The first thing that a Facebook user looks at every time they enter into their personal Facebook account.

2. It is the place where a Facebook user receives every single post, video, image, etc. that their Facebook friends haves posted into their own Facebook accounts, as well as all the posts, videos and images from all the Facebook Pages they have liked.

3. It is one of the most seen places of the entire Facebook Personal Account by every Facebook User.

2. Viral Effect:

The great thing about a post is that once your friends see the post they can do 3 actions: Like, Comment or Share, making the post amazingly viral.

If your friends click on any of those buttons, their friends will receive a notification about it, and if the friends of your friends do the same, the viral effect is then taking place, with just a simple and single post.

3. Pin to Top:

This function is amazingly great. It consist on the possibility to place your post in the top of your posts for 7 days, so those people that are visiting your Facebook Page interface may see it right away.

4. Share your Post:

Another great way to have more exposure to your post is to "Share" it using the "Share" feature located in your own post.

The options are self-explanatory. I just want to point out that on the first one, you will be able to post that same post on your own Facebook Personal Account Timeline (or News Feed) so all of your friends (including the ones that have not liked your Page jet) may see your post too.

5. Boost Post:

This feature will help your post go viral a lot faster and wither.

The crazy great thing about this is that that Boost will not go to a bunch of people that are not interested in knowing about your

Facebook Page. That Boost will go to the people that have liked your page, but have not seen your post, as well as all of their friends, which certainly can be people with the same likes as your friends.

6. Tips and Guidelines:

It is obvious to tell you this but it is important to remind you that you really need to post something of value. If you go to your own Facebook Personal Account News Feed, you can see everything your friends are sharing with you, pay close attention on those posts that entice you to like, comment or even share it with your own friends. Take those attractive posts as an example for your postings. The purpose of your post is not to get just views, you want people to click on it, like it, comment on it, and even share it with others.

Please think before deciding to "Pin" a post; that post will stay in the top for 7 days and if your friends don't like it, it is so easy to get them to unlike your page just like it is to get them like it. You can pin a product launch, and product update, a testimonial for customers will be great to pin, a really cool valuable video, a picture, a contest, an offer, etc. just avoid regular posts in this spot.

The average life of a post on Facebook is around 3 to 4 hours.

Questions are good to make people respond (comment) on your post.

Do not post like crazy, it is really annoying, and people will start un-liking you ad even un-friending you.

Strongly advise you to create a post experiment for views. You can post every day, but on a different hour; in that way you can see when people usually get into their Facebook accounts because the post will be in front of them right away.

Now that you know at what time to post, you may pay attention on a post experiment for likes, comments and shares at the same time. In that way you will know your audience really well and avoid un-likes gaining more interactions.

Adjust your posting to them as much as possible.

Do some research online and if you find any report, video, training or software freely available to get and completely related to your Facebook Page topic; that will be great to share. Your audience will start finding your Facebook Page useful enough to care about it once you send them a new post.

Get the most advantage of the short text posts. Posts between 100 and 250 characters (less than 3 lines of text) see about 60% more likes, comments and shares than posts greater than 250 characters.

And finally, we will guide you to get as many likes as possible to your brand new Facebook Page so you may get the most out of this amazing technology and super viral social advertising power.

Step 8: Getting Likes… quickly and safely…

You may have the greatest Facebook Page in the world but with no "likes" you are lost. But first of all, let me explain the power that is within a Facebook Page Like.

An opt in form has the purpose of collecting the contact information of as many people as possible, thus creating what is called a "List," so the administrator of the opting form may contact everyone in the "List" by email using an email auto-responder service. This is what is called Email Marketing.

On the other hand, the "like" button will give the ability to your friends and visitors to be part of a list as well, a list of people who like your page. So the administrator of the Facebook Page may contact them directly into their "News Feed" that the user checks very often, and (in my opinion) more often than their email accounts.

The purpose is the same. Contact or send a message to a list of people that have decided to accept information from the administrator of the option form or Facebook Page. But there are a lot of very important differences that I really want to point out here.

ABOUT THE AUTHOR

Steven Murphy is one of those young businessmen that have a vast range of new ideas, self-driven with a mind of a goal getter. Steven readily understood that there is a likeable profit in doing marketing through Facebook. He then tried it for himself and gets more than likeable result.

Steven Murphy is also a financial adviser and consultant in many firms. Steven developed several platforms for beginning business as well and help them attract more customers.

www.ingramcontent.com/pod-product-compliance
Lightning Source LLC
Chambersburg PA
CBHW070900070326
40690CB00009B/1929